Morning Glory

Morning Glory

Haiku and tanka
by
Alan Spence

Illustrated by
Elizabeth Blackadder

Elizabeth Blackadder

Collected and edited by Lucina Prestige

Renaissance Press

First published in 2010
2nd edition 2011
by
Renaissance Press
4 Warriston Crescent
Edinburgh EH3 5LA

ISBN 978-0-954-3961-2-1

Printed by Stewarts of Edinburgh

Acknowledgements

Some of these poems first appeared in *Edinburgh Review*, *Island*, *Panorama*, *The Thing That Mattered Most* (Scottish Poetry Library) and *Urthona*.

Other books from Renaissance Press

Through the Letterbox by George Bruce, illustrated by Elizabeth Blackadder (2003)
The Singing of the Foxes by George Bruce, illustrations by John Bellany (2007)

Introduction

'Haiku is a kind of painting' said Duncan Macmillan (art historian and art critic) in his introduction to *The Scottish Gallery's* Edinburgh Festival Exhibition catalogue of 1998. This was for an exhibition of paintings by Elizabeth Blackadder. 'She is in her own way a haiku painter'.

And what more perfect collaboration could there be than the master of Scottish haiku writing, Alan Spence, combined with the sensitivity and delicacy of Elizabeth Blackadder's painting?

This book of haiku (and the occasional tanka) is the product of many years of labour, contemplation and affection. In it, the reader will find much to amuse and delight, but also plenty to prompt reflection - and admiration for the author and the artist's extraordinary creative skills.

The peacock screeches,
shrieks me awake.
Look. See. His
iridescent feathers
are God's-eye blue.

In memory of

Sri Chinmoy
1931 - 2007

and

John Houston RSA
1930 - 2008

in silence, out of
the falling snow,
a swan, flying

dog on the roof
of his kennel
barking at the day

10

it was *this* big!
the child tells her mother,
on the phone

It's just the way
these lambs newborn
in simple lambness know
exactly how to be
what just they are.

walking meditation
one foot after the other
consciously

half-closing my eyes
to see the flowers
more clearly

a single pink
umbrella
in the spring rain

snow in may?
flurry of cherry blossoms
falling

From far away we see
the mountain clear;
up close it dis-
    appears completely
in the mist.

the mist clears
and, briefly, the mountain
is there

sun after rain
after sun after
rain

blue hills beyond
blue hills
beyond blue hills

The peacock screeches,
shrieks me awake.
Look. See. His
iridescent feathers
are God's-eye blue.

that sweet cacophony
these chirping birds
this clear morning

morning meditation
breathe in / breathe out
waves on the shore

in the silence
after chanting mantras –
birdsong

Wind, water, mind,
all of it moving,
the river a torrent.
Midstream on a rock,
the heron, poised and still.

intoxicating
that coconut scent
of yellow gorse

I can't help it –
asking the morning glory
what's the story?

stray dog eating
the offering left out
for the gods

numbing heat –
the old dog strains
to mark his territory

the night gets hotter –
hazy moon through
the mosquito-screen

At the temple
to Kwan-Yin,
goddess of mercy,
trying not to step
on the ants.

this other element –
swimming in the sea
in the rain

letting go of all
the misery – swimming
in the ocean

swimming in the ocean –
catching the wave,
being caught by it

A Chinese temple
willowpattern blue –
my father's bar of
chocolate ginger,
Glasgow 1959.

all day downpour –
flooded gutters,
stink of blocked drains

watching
the sky darkening,
the moon brightening

Middle of the night –
the thin time
between worlds.
The blinds are open.
The moonlight streams in.

white mare in the rain,
placid, feeding
her guzzling foal

Cutting through
their conversation,
the blind man passes
between them, tap
tapping his cane.

so still, this
northern halflight
this *simmerdim*

fallen petals
swirled up by the wind
dancing

indian summer –
the great bull
lying on his side

3am – *Brahma muhurta,*
the hour of the gods.
Unable to sleep,
I face my demons with
meditation and green tea.

distant star
fading as the sky
lightens

over the wall
of the cemetery –
sunflowers

in the middle
of the funeral
the child's laugh

each leaf as it falls
catches
        a moment
    the light

Mahasamadhi -
my master's passing.
My own gratitude-heart,
we sing, is all
that matters.

after his passing,
everything as it was,
nothing as it was

Turned inside out
by an old song
on the radio -
Something changed....
It did, forever.

it's the autumn wind
that blows these leaves
over his grave

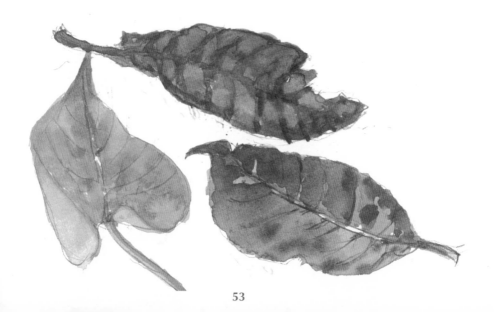

after the funeral
blue blue blue
those morning glories

and my life too
is passing – evening light
on the far mountains

An understanding
of resurrection –
the way his light
burns bright in me
after his passing.

To have lived
so many lives –
how many loves
I know but
do not know.

not this not this
but still that old
familiar moon

waking from a dream
of rain falling
to rain, falling

You burn pine incense
in Kamakura –
I catch its scent
in Edinburgh
this autumn afternoon.

footballers training
in the autumn rain –
the new season

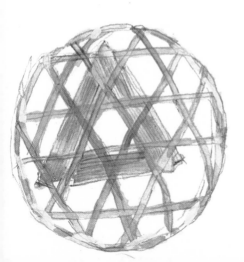

scrabbling, a mouse
behind the skirting board –
cold october night

why this? why that?
all night the rain
on fallen leaves

jetlagged in japan –
forgetting, remembering
who I am

middle of the night
the traffic lights changing
for no-one

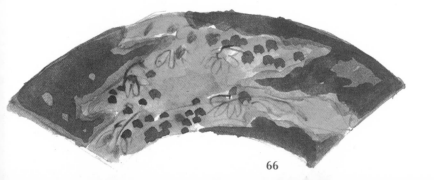

the sea at night
wave after wave
out of the dark

First time in China –
feels like returning
after lifetimes away.
Above the traffic noise,
a nightingale, singing.

The cabaret singers
pack up for the night.
Out in the bay,
the lights
of the fishing boats.

night-fishing
each boat in the circle
of its own light

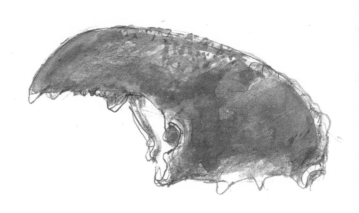

washed up on the shore
an empty bottle
no message

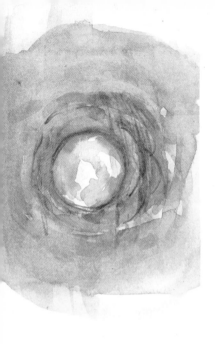

checking the calendar
to make sure, but
yes, the moon's full!

Lingering,
the scent of
that young girl
long after she's
passed me by.

Her hair still damp
from the shower,
she hurries out
to meet her lover,
feels the autumn chill.

Hopefully, she says
into her cellphone
in the busy city street.
Yes, she says, with all
her heart. *Absolutely.*

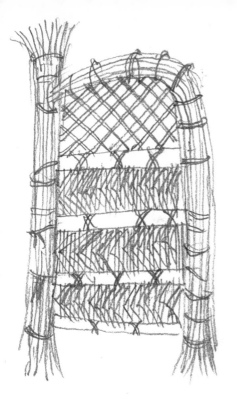

at the temple gate
in concentrated silence
the stone lion roars

Last quarter, last third
of my life? Either way
it's autumn,
shading, shading
into winter.

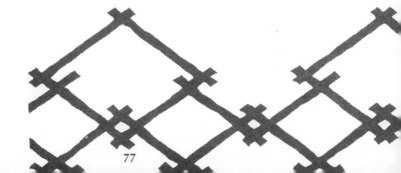

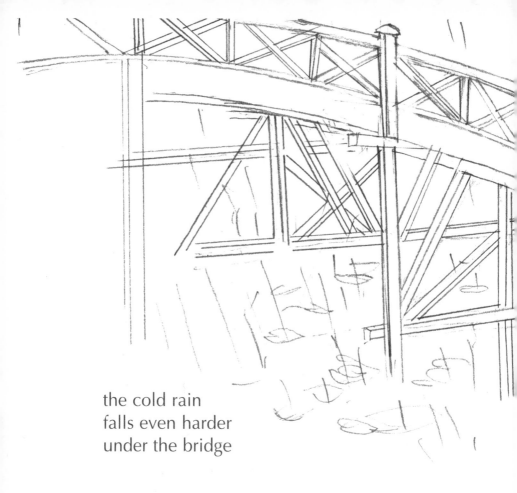

the cold rain
falls even harder
under the bridge

dark already –
the icy rain
incessant

In the fading light
the blind woman smiles
to herself,
reading with her
          fingertips.

that winter smell –
old towel drying
on the radiator

winter – the cat
clawing to get out,
clawing to get back in

not light till nine /
dark again at four /
and in between / rain

another birthday –
never mind the cold,
fling the window open!

My name in the book –
year of my birth,
a hyphen and then
that blank space waiting
to be filled in.

bright winter morning –
how simple it all seems,
how clear

so far north –
this light so
clear so blue

so cold –
tying my shoelaces
with gloved hands

And then it will be
over, as over as it is for
Shakespeare, Mozart, Lao Tsu,
my mother and father and all
the rest.

out of season
the hotel swimming pool
frozen over

Will this thick ice
take my weight?
One foot. The other.
Hear it start
    to crack

december dusk –
the dog's harsh bark
deepens the cold

This cold dark morning
awake and listening,
listening to
the sound of
the unseen ocean.

it fades, it fades,
the last light
of the year

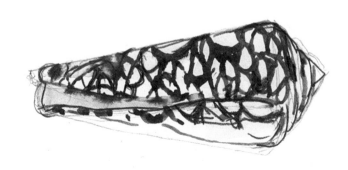

new year dawn
red sun rising
out of the black sea

overnight snow
crystallized into
iceflowers

snow on snow
making
not a sound

in the snow
the fox and I, startled
by each other

new year's morning –
above the rooftops
a line of white smoke

new year – my neighbour
has painted his front door
bright blue

Let it all go. The new
year enters. The earth
turns in space. The waves
crash on the shore.
Let it all go.